Pauls Final Words To the Church
Letter of 2nd Timothy

ISBN979-8-89145-411-8
(Paper Back)
Book Design and Story by Don Pirozok
Editor Cheryl Pirozok

First Printing 2023 Amazon Publishing, United States

Contents

Pauls Final Words To the Church
The Letter of 2nd Timothy

Chapter One: Paul and Timothy

The apostle Pauls final words to the Church are written in his letter to his young apostle team member Timothy. Paul gives out his final insight concerning Church issues, Church leadership, and the future direction of the Church. The apostle Paul develops in greater detail about his concerns which was briefly recorded in the book of Acts.

Acts 20:22-31
22 And now, behold, I go bound in the spirit unto Jerusalem, not knowing the things that shall befall me there:
23 Save that the Holy Ghost witnesseth in every city, saying that bonds and afflictions abide me.
24 But none of these things move me, neither count I my life dear unto myself, so that I might finish my course with joy, and the ministry, which I have received of the Lord Jesus, to testify the gospel of the grace of God.
25 And now, behold, I know that ye all, among whom I have gone preaching the kingdom of God, shall see my face no more.
26 Wherefore I take you to record this day, that I am pure from the blood of all men.

27 For I have not shunned to declare unto you all the
counsel of God.
28 Take heed therefore unto yourselves, and to all the
flock, over the which the Holy Ghost hath made you
overseers, to feed the church of God, which he hath
purchased with his own blood.
29 For I know this, that after my departing shall grievous
wolves enter in among you, not sparing the flock.
30 Also of your own selves shall men arise, speaking
perverse things, to draw away disciples after them.
31 Therefore watch, and remember, that by the space
of three years I ceased not to warn every one night and
day with tears.

Paul knew his future of arrest and eventual martyrdom, and knew more trouble was coming to the Church. As Gnostic false prophets were already active in the Church bringing in their doctrines of the demons. Also, Paul was already exposing the presence of false apostles who were bringing into the Church what Paul identified as another Jesus, by another Gospel, by a false Holy Spirit. All those situations were already happening, now Paul is going to his own death at the hands of Rome. With Pauls departure he warns of corruption from within the Church coming from the Church leaders themselves who would draw men away from Jesus Christ unto their own agendas. Also false prophets would arise as devouring wolves from within their own ranks not sparing the flock. It seems like he is passing the torch unto one of his fellow apostolic leaders whom Paul is giving final instructions and warnings.

Paul first identifies his calling and work in the Lord, as the Lord's apostle. To Pauls spiritual son and also to the Church of Jesus Christ. For whatever Paul speaks He speaks on behalf of the Lord by inspiration of the Holy Spirit. Paul said his conscience was clear even though he was formerly a great persecutor of the Church before his conversion in Christ. Paul calls for grace, mercy and peace which comes God our Father and His Son, Jesus Christ. Of course, the Gnostic false prophets denied the Incarnation of Jesus Christ, and God the Father of the Lord Jesus Christ. Paul was in deep prayer for Timothy, as Paul was likely in prison when this letter was written to Timothy, and Paul longed to see Timothy again. Paul was convinced of the sincerity of Timothy's devotion to Jesus Christ since his early childhood.

2 Timothy 1:1-5
1 Paul, an apostle of Jesus Christ by the will of God, according to the promise of life which is in Christ Jesus,
2 To Timothy, my dearly beloved son: Grace, mercy, and peace, from God the Father and Christ Jesus our Lord.
3 I thank God, whom I serve from my forefathers with pure conscience, that without ceasing I have remembrance of thee in my prayers night and day;
4 Greatly desiring to see thee, being mindful of thy tears, that I may be filled with joy;

5 When I call to remembrance the unfeigned faith that
is in thee, which dwelt first in thy grandmother Lois, and
thy mother Eunice; and I am persuaded that in thee
also.

Paul being in prison under Roman guard reminded Timothy not to be afraid of the testimony of Jesus Christ. Paul was exhorting Timothy the cost of preaching the true word of God, the Gospel of Jesus Christ. In the face of great persecution even under the threat of his life, Paul reminds Timothy not to fear man's persecutions. As God has given His Holy Spirit, and not a spirit of fear, but a spirit of power, love, and a sound mind.

7 For God hath not given us the spirit of fear; but of
power, and of love, and of a sound mind.
8 Be not thou therefore ashamed of the testimony of
our Lord, nor of me his prisoner: but be thou partaker of
the afflictions of the gospel according to the power of
God;
9 Who hath saved us, and called us with a holy calling,
not according to our works, but according to tohis own
purpose and grace, which was given us in Christ Jesus
before the world began,
10 But is now made manifest by the appearing of our
Saviour Jesus Christ, who hath abolished death, and
hath brought life and immortality to light through the
gospel:

Paul reminds Timothy God has given them the Gospel of Grace to preach, not according to the works of man, but was already given in the person of Jesus Christ before the world began. Now that Jesus Christ has already come, our Savior Jesus Christ by His Cross and Resurrection has brought life and immortality to light through the Gospel.

Who Is Apostle Timothy
"Timothy or Timothy of Ephesus (Greek: Τιμόθεος; Timótheos, meaning "honouring God" or "honoured by God"[8]) was an early Christian evangelist and the first Christian bishop of Ephesus,[9] who tradition relates died around the year AD 97.
Timothy was from the Lycaonian city of Lystra[10] or of Derbe[2][3] in Asia Minor, born of a Jewish mother who had become a Christian believer, and a Greek father. The Apostle Paul met him during his second missionary journey and he became Paul's companion and missionary partner along with Silas.[11] The New Testament indicates that Timothy traveled with Paul the Apostle, who was also his mentor. He is addressed as the recipient of the First and Second Epistles to Timothy. While included in the Pauline epistles of the New Testament, First and Second Timothy are considered by many biblical scholars to be pseudo epigraphical and not written by Paul." Wikipedia

Timothy was a native of Lystra or of Derbe in Lycaonia (Anatolia).[12] When Paul and Barnabas first visited

Lystra, Paul healed a person crippled from birth, leading many of the inhabitants to accept his teaching. When he returned a few years later with Silas, Timothy was already a respected member of the Christian congregation, as were his grandmother Lois and his mother Eunice, both Jews. In 2 Timothy 1:5,[13] his mother and grandmother are noted as eminent for their piety and faith. Timothy is said to have been acquainted with the Scriptures since childhood. In 1 Corinthians 16:10,[14] there is a suggestion that he was by nature reserved and timid: "When Timothy comes, see that you put him at ease among you, for he is doing the work of the Lord".[15]

Timothy's father was a Greek Gentile. Thus, Timothy had not been circumcised and Paul now ensured that this was done, according to Acts 16:1-3,[16] to ensure Timothy's acceptability to the Jews whom they would be evangelizing. According to John William McGarvey:[17] "Yet we see him in the case before us, circumcising Timothy with his own hand, and this 'on account of certain Jews who were in those quarters'". This did not compromise the decision made at the Council of Jerusalem, that gentile believers were not required to be circumcised. [citation needed]

Timothy became St Paul's disciple, and later his constant companion and co-worker in preaching.[18] In the year 52, Paul and Silas took Timothy along with them on their journey to Macedonia. Augustine extols his zeal and disinterestedness in immediately forsaking his country, his house, and his parents, to follow the apostle, to share in his poverty and sufferings.[19] Timothy may have been subject to ill health or "frequent ailments", and Paul encouraged him to "use a little wine for your stomach's sake".[20]

When Paul went on to Athens, Silas and Timothy stayed for some time at Beroea and Thessalonica before joining Paul at Corinth.[19] 1 Thessalonians 3:1–6 suggests that from Corinth, Paul sent Timothy back to Thessalonika to enquire about the community's continued faith, reporting back that it was in good shape. Timothy next appears in Acts during Paul's stay in Ephesus (54–57), and in late 56 or early 57 Paul sent him forth to Macedonia with the aim that he would eventually arrive at Corinth. Timothy arrived at Corinth just after Paul's letter 1 Corinthians reached that city. [citation needed]

Timothy was with Paul in Corinth during the winter of 57–58 when Paul dispatched his Letter to the Romans.[21] According to Acts 20:3–6,[22] Timothy was with Paul in Macedonia just before Passover in 58; he left the city before Paul, going ahead of him to await Paul in Troas.[23] "That is the last mention of Timothy in Acts", Raymond Brown notes.[24] In the year 64, Paul left Timothy at Ephesus, to govern that church.[19]
His relationship with Paul was close. Timothy's name appears as the co-author on 2 Corinthians, Philippians, Colossians, 1 Thessalonians, 2 Thessalonians, and

Philemon. Paul wrote to the Philippians about Timothy, "I have no one like him."[25] When Paul was in prison and awaiting martyrdom, he summoned his faithful friend Timothy for a last farewell.[18]
That Timothy was jailed at least once during the period of the writing of the New Testament is implied by the writer of Hebrews mentioning Timothy's release at the end of the epistle.[26]
Although not stated in the New Testament, other sources have records of the apostle's death. The apocryphal Acts of Timothy states that in the year 97 AD, the 80-year-old bishop tried to halt a procession in honor of the goddess Diana by preaching the Gospel. The angry pagans beat him, dragged him through the streets, and stoned him to death (Wikipedia)

Hold Fast Sound Words

The apostle Paul in his first letter to Timothy was emphasizing qualifications for a church leaders. In this second letter Paul further develops his concern for Church leaders, and men who don't qualify and Church leaders who fail to keep the true Gospel of Jesus Christ. Paul begins to lay out for Timothy the importance of contending for the faith an watching over the words you are speaking on behalf of the Lord God.

2 Timothy 1:13-14
13 Hold fast the form of sound words, which thou hast heard of me, in faith and love which is in Christ Jesus.

14 That good thing which was committed unto thee keep by the Holy Ghost which dwelleth in us.

Sound words which Jesus Christ had taught the apostle Paul which today we know as the Gospel of Grace. It was contrary to the works of the law and was the source of much contention among the Jews, even those who had been born again by grace by added the law. The cost by which Paul has to pay meant times would have to stand alone being abandoned by those who should have stood with Paul in times of persecution.

One brother in Christ however sought out Paul in his imprisonment, and brought necessary comfort to Paul in standing, with him in times of suffering. Others Paul identified by name who ran from the cost, and Paul was asking for Gods upon them at the Judgment Seat of Christ. Where all Christians have to give an account for how they served the Lord, or how they did not serve the Lord.
2 Timothy 1:15-18
15 This thou knowest, that all they which are in Asia be turned away from me; of whom are Phygellus and Hermogenes.
16 The Lord give mercy unto the house of Onesiphorus; for he oft refreshed me, and was not ashamed of my chain:
17 But, when he was in Rome, he sought me out very diligently, and found me.

18 The Lord grant unto him that he may find mercy of the Lord in that day: and in how many things he ministered unto me at Ephesus, thou knowest very well.

Chapter Two: Pauls Defense of the Faith

The apostle Paul then further develops the thought of serving the Lord faithfully. Paul speaks to Timothy like a spiritual father to accept the grace of God upon his life and be strong in the Lord by walking out that grace. Paul then wants Timothy to take the things he has learned and heard from Paul and give them to other men who are also walking, out their callings in faithful obedience to the Lord. Paul wanted Timothy to disciple other leaders who then would take from Timothy and teach other men. In this way a great multiplication of new leaders and new disciples could result.
2 Timothy 2:1-4
1 Thou therefore, my son, be strong in the grace that is in Christ Jesus.
2 And the things that thou hast heard of me among many witnesses, the same commit thou to faithful men, who shall be able to teach others also.
3 Thou therefore endure hardness, as a good soldier of Jesus Christ.
4 No man that warreth entangleth himself with the affairs of this life; that he may please him who hath chosen him to be a soldier.

The Good Solder of Jesus Christ

In 2 Timothy we are given a picture of faithful stewards in Christ who are walking, out their callings and election in the Lord in Church leadership. Paul comes this rigorous life of severe to those who are in the military trained to be soldiers. Not that the Christian faith is to be a militant aggressive personality, rather it's a submissive dedication to the service to which he has been enlisted. In many way a solider has given up his rights to a civilian life and is in constant vigilance being prepared to defend his nation. The training and the lifestyle of a solider requires a great amount of devotion in which the common civilian does not have to live. Many would say a soldiers life is one of strict observance to the directions of his commanders, and many times soldiers are put into conditions in which they must endure many hostile environments.

Paul is appealing to the apostle Timothy to see how Gods call upon his life is similar to a soldiers life, and Timothy must endure many difficult afflictions. As a good solider of Jesus Christ God call men into his service at the cost of their connivence and easy life.

Timothy as the Lords solider must entangle himself in many unnecessary things of this life which would pull him away from the soldiers dedication. Now no man who goes to war is being entangled by the affairs of this life, but is devoted to the warfare at hand. A dedicated solider is following commands of his generals and in so doing earns a high degree of rewards from the military. Even so will it be with soldiers in Christ who are pleasing to the Lord. They will earn a high degree of rewards at the Second Coming of Jesus Christ.

Gods Farmer

Paul further develops the sense of future rewards obtained by faithful service to Jesus Christ during one's lifetime. If a man seeks to be a master, an expert at what he does and the be rewarded for all his effort and training, he is not rewarded by others unless the conditions of his mastery were legally obtained. So will it be with Jesus Christ at the Judgment Seat of Christ where the Lord will reward every man according to their works without prejudice or partiality.

2 Timothy 2:5-7

5 And if a man also strive for masteries, yet is he not crowned, except he strive lawfully.

6 The husbandman that laboureth must be first partaker of the fruits.

7 Consider what I say; and the Lord give thee understanding in all things.

Now let us consider the master farmer who has become an expert in growing the crops or raising the flocks which has brought great results. Seeing the farmer will be the first to experience the fruit of his labor being directly involved in the actual farming day in and day out operations. The farmer himself will be the first to see and experience the fruits of his labors. While after others will be benefited from all his expertise and work. In the same way faithful servants of the Lord who have faithful grown in the mastery of their calling in Christ will be considered by the Lord to partake first of the Lords highest rewards. If even now many men in their search for a lawful crowning from the Lord at His Second Coming must suffer great loss of the things of this present age. Simply put the Lord will not crown a man who has not attained to the Crown, neither will He without the Crown from one who in the eyes of the world was a fool for God. Notice how God has chosen the weak and foolish things in the eyes of the world to confound the wise and mighty of the world.

Paul goes on to develop how God servants must suffer injustices in this age while serving the Lord, but will be rewarded the Crown upon the Lords return. Jesus serves as our example even though he was the king he suffered shame and reproach in order to qualify for the Crown. In a similar way Paul reminds Timothy Christ is the Son of David legal heir to the Throne but was never crowned by the people of this age. However, Jesus Christ fully obeyed the Father even unto the death of the Cross, wherefore God has highly exalted Him and given Him a name above every name.

Paul reminds Timothy how he was falsely charged and imprisoned for doing what was right in the eyes of God. In this world however, Paul was treated with hostilities which men did calling Paul a troubler and an evil man. Even Paul is his striving for the Lords mastery must suffer this reproach being imprisoned, but his passion was to serve the Lord for the elect sakes. Willing to

suffer loss in his own personal life so they may obtain the salvation which give them eternal glory in Christ. Paul would be made the offscouring of the world a fool for Christ, that others may come to know the glory of God for their lives.
2 Timothy 2:8-13
8 Remember that Jesus Christ of the seed of David was raised from the dead according to my gospel:
9 Wherein I suffer trouble, as an evil doer, even unto bonds; but the word of God is not bound.
10 Therefore I endure all things for the elect's sakes, that they may also obtain the salvation which is in Christ Jesus with eternal glory.
11 It is a faithful saying: For if we be dead with him, we shall also live with him:
12 If we suffer, we shall also reign with him: if we deny him, he also will deny us:
13 If we believe not, yet he abideth faithful: he cannot deny himself.

Now comes Paul wisdom regarding the value in the fellowship of the suffering of Jesus Christ. Paul sees what suffering in service to the Lord God results, "if we be dead with Him we shall also live with Him, if we suffer we shall also reign with Him, now if we pull back in denial being afraid of the cost of suffering and deny the Lord, He will, refuse us at the Judgment Seat of Christ disqualifying us from the Crown. However, if we abide in unbelief, it will never change the Lord as He ever abides faithful. For the Lord God could never deny

Himself. We see the faithful witness while on trial at the Cross when He did not deny He is the Son of God. A confession which sent Jesus Christ to the Cross.

Gods Workman
2 Peter 2:14-18
14 Of these things put them in remembrance, charging them before the Lord that they strive not about words to no profit, but to the subverting of the hearers.
15 Study to shew thyself approved unto God, a workman that needeth not to be ashamed, rightly dividing the word of truth.
16 But shun profane and vain babblings: for they will increase unto more ungodliness.
17 And their word will eat as doth a canker: of whom is Hymenaeus and Philetus;
18 Who concerning the truth have erred, saying that the resurrection is past already; and overthrow the faith of some.

Now comes so very sober realities of failed Church leaders, and the false doctrines they teach. What do false teaches do to the Church? The bring about schisms, divisions in the body of Christ where men strive against one another. False words subvert the hearers, meaning it creates a move towards apostasy in the faith. It is to be treated with an inmost urgency by those who teach Gods children. You are to study to show yourselves approved by God, as Gods workman laboring in the Church correctly. A workman who by diligent study knows how to rightly divide the doctrines of Jesus Christ and not bring the shame of schisms upon the Church. A man who can by reason of use rightly divide Gods word of righteousness, and knows the difference between the milk of the word, and the meat of God's word.

All this noise in the modern Church we those who speak in the name of the Lord bring in their own subjectivity and personal revelations which leads the Church away from the Lord unto more ungodliness. Back in the apostles Pauls day two men named by Paul as false teachers were overthrowing the faith of some Christians by saying the resurrection is already past. Meaning Jesus Christ had already come for the Church and all these we left behind, and the dead were already with the Lord. Not that there was no resurrection, instead proclaiming a false timing of the resurrection of the saints teaching it had already happened. Paul said this doctrine of demons was eating at the Church like a deadly cancer making the body of Christ sick with demonic deception.

Today is certain segments of the Church we have men and women who are called Preterism who proclaim there is no need for a bodily Second Coming of Jesus Christ. In this way they also deny the future Second Coming of Jesus Christ and the raising of the saints from death into immortality by a bodily resurrection of their own. This doctrine is growing in popularity as the

Church is showing more signs of apostasy from the true doctrines of Jesus Christ. As they embrace a false resurrection so also is the denial of the Cross by proclaiming a Universal Salvation for all mankind. A denial of eternal damnation in the Lake of Fire, and all men saved out of Hell even if in their lifetimes they rebelled against salvation in Jesus Christ.

How dangerous are the false doctrines and false teachers of todays organized Church. How popular have many become as the Church has been seduced to follow their private interpretations of the Word of God which violate what true doctrines actually teach.

Why Is the Resurrection of Jesus Christ the proof of the Christian faith

I consider Good Friday and the next three days the foundation of the Christian faith. Good Friday the day the Lord was crucified for the sins of the world. The three days of Christ's soul descended into Hades, and the resurrection from out among the dead. However, the Scriptures do highlight the day of the Lords resurrection from the dead as uniquely important for Christians, and for saints of God throughout the history of the world. The apostle Paul explains the significance of the Resurrection of Jesus Christ;

1 Corinthians 15:12-19
12 Now if Christ be preached that he rose from the

dead, how say some among you that there is no
resurrection of the dead?
13 But if there be no resurrection of the dead, then is
Christ not risen:
14 And if Christ be not risen, then is our preaching vain,
and your faith is also vain.
15 Yea, and we are found false witnesses of God;
because we have testified of God that he raised up
Christ: whom he raised not up, if so be that the dead
rise not.
16 For if the dead rise not, then is not Christ raised:
17 And if Christ be not raised, your faith is vain; ye are
yet in your sins.
18 Then they also which are fallen asleep in Christ are
perished.
19 If in this life only we have hope in Christ, we are of all
men most miserable.

What is Paul saying? If in this life is the Christian faith only, then Christians are of all men the most miserable. For those who died in Christ have perished, never to be reunited with their bodies, subjected to deaths dominion living in a cursed state for all eternity. Do you not understand if Christ has not risen from the dead then Christian faith is in vain. Basically, an empty profession having very little substance as nothing really has changed concerning the corruption of our bodies and corruption in the world. In Paul's words if there be no resurrection lets us eat and drink for tomorrow we die. What does the failure of the resurrection mean?

We are still in your sins, and death will be master in the end. If we are only born again in this life, and then die with no hope of resurrection no salvation from sin and death really exists. No is only glorified when his body is raised from the dead in resurrection. As the state of death is not the state of glorification, it is the result of being cursed by sin and death. A very powerful deception has befallen humanity to think glory is upon death. As more men will die and go to Hell and suffer in Hell Fire in a disembodied state of death.

So what is the Christian faith based upon? The resurrection of Jesus Christ from among the dead. Why is the most important of days and events in the Christian faith. It is proof the Blood Sacrifice of Jesus Christ paid the debit to sin, and was perfect without blemish having no sin. Man declared Jesus Christ guilty of committing blasphemy professing He is the Son of God. However, they could not convict Him of any sin. When Christ was crucified He did not die for His own sins, instead was made to be sin, a sacrifice for the sin of the world. If the life of Christ was not sinless, not perfect, then sin and death has a rightful claim on Christ's life and there would be no resurrection of Jesus Christ from the dead. Christ died for our sin, and was raised for our justification.

Meaning the resurrection is proof the blood of Jesus Christ opened up acceptance before God and opened the grave in power over sin and death. The resurrection

of Jesus Christ is proof the Blood Sacrifice of Jesus Christ has been accepted by God paying the way for our eternal salvation. Which would have to include our own resurrection from the dead, and made immortal and glorified in our own resurrection bodies. Jesus Christ is the first born from the dead, a forerunner who has paid the way for our future Day of Redemption which is the day of our resurrection out from among the dead.
The whole of the Christian faith is based upon Jesus Christ's resurrection from among the dead. Followed by our resurrection from among the dead. Right now, we are sealed in our mortal bodies by the Holy Spirit if so be you have been saved by faith. When you die your hope remains in Christ's power to raise the dead. His own resurrection demonstrates in Jesus Christ alone is immortality and eternal life. As all other men who are great religious leaders, Muhammad, Buddha, Confucius, Gandhi, Joseph Smith, and others are still in their graves. For there is salvation in no other name other than the name of Jesus Christ. No other man has said, "I Am the Resurrection and the life."

John 11:17-26
17 Then when Jesus came, he found that he had lain in the grave four days already.
18 Now Bethany was nigh unto Jerusalem, about fifteen furlongs off:
19 And many of the Jews came to Martha and Mary, to comfort them concerning their brother.

20 Then Martha, as soon as she heard that Jesus was
coming, went and met him: but Mary sat still in the
house.
21 Then said Martha unto Jesus, Lord, if thou hadst
been here, my brother had not died.
22 But I know, that even now, whatsoever thou wilt ask
of God, God will give it thee.
23 Jesus saith unto her, Thy brother shall rise again.
24 Martha saith unto him, I know that he shall rise again
in the resurrection at the last day.
25 Jesus said unto her, I am the resurrection, and the
life: he that believeth in me, though he were dead, yet
shall he live:
26 And whosoever liveth and believeth in me shall
never die. Believest thou this?

Satan's War on the Gospel

I find it ironic some much attention is given to spiritual warfare in the Charismatic Movement, while at the same time deny Satan s main strategy of deception. All manner of techniques like casting down dark angels from their rule over the 7 pillars of culture or putting Satan on trial in the courts of heaven. While falling to the most basic form of Satan s warfare by attacking the Gospel.

A simple question must be asked, with all the super spiritual sophistication going on in the Charismatic Movement, why the lack of understanding concerning "Satan s attack on the Gospel?" The answer is quite

simple, but unwanted as a reason by many who are defending the Charismatic Movement, many who are the "super apostles of the Charismatic Movement" are the chief offenders in preaching a false Gospel. Which means these Charismatic leaders do not have the true maturity to see what they are preaching is not coming from the Word of God. Since Satan has attacked the Word of God from the beginning "why hasn't warnings of deception in false doctrines come from Charismatic leaders?"
What are the three primary ways Satan attacks the Word of God? In the Church Satan has sown an "another Gospel, by "another spirit," with false messengers." The difficulty being it looks like the authentic Gospel, or the historic Jesus, or the Holy Spirit, but its Satan's imitation. Yes, the name of Jesus is used, or the love of God, even forgiveness and miracles. Its nearly right, but not right. It's another Gospel, a lot like the original, it sounds good, but its Satan's Gospel. That's what makes it so evil, because it looks like light, but its pure darkness. Without your senses trained to discern good and evil which comes from spiritual maturity knowing the meat of the Word, Satan leads Charismatics to following a false Gospel.

What is the problem of following another Gospel? When a Christian point out it is not the doctrine of Jesus Christ, whose word do you trust. The only true measure is to take both views of what is being preached and measure it by the written Word of God. In true spiritual warfare Satan quotes the Scripture but has twisted its true meaning. So following a man who is popular, or successful, is likely to get you into deep waters of deception. The only true remedy in spiritual warfare is to "speak the word only," if the popular man cannot truly defend his doctrines by the written Word of God, you will end up following a false messenger.

Charismatics must understand Satan's false Gospel must be preached by a "false messenger." The False Gospel, and another Jesus just don't happen on their own. Satan must have a messenger inside the Church in order to preach or teach. Does a false messenger then make them a Satan worshiper? The answer is also simple but unwanted by many who refuse to hear. Most of the men and women are "nearly apostles, or nearly prophets," but preach and teach false doctrines. So, this makes them a false messenger who has fallen to the wiles of Satan. They are nearly apostles, nearly prophets, or teachers but in fact are false apostles, false prophets, or false teachers. Satan has false apostles in the Church by reason of their willingness to preach Satan's false Gospel, it's that simple.
It's not just eating the wheat, and then spitting out the chaff. It's another Gospel, with another Jesus which leads to Satan's deception. The result of exalting men and women who falsely teach and preach the written word of God. Without admitting this basic spiritual warfare, Satan has sown his Gospel inside the Church for nearly two thousand years.

Naming False Teachers

So, one might ask why name names? Let's say you have a major heresy being taught like Jesus Christ is not God while being a man on earth. That heresy has become quite popular among Charismatics who believe in miracles, as it is used to teach all Christians can do what Jesus did. As Jesus Christ laid aside His divinity and only did miracles as a man and not God. This is a blatant doctrine of demons known as the Kenosis heresy and has been clearly exposed in Church history and by Church Fathers. So even though its heretical it's still popular among modern day Charismatics, do Christians who are contending for the faith have a right to expose the "Kenosis heresy?" Most everyone would agree you do have a right to "expose heresies and doctrines of demons." Why? Its damaging to the authentic Christian faith, like a cancer wanting to eat away at the health of the body.

Many Charismatics who hold to the Kenosis Heresy will simply argue that they don't agree, and they hold to their position or won't comment at all. However, when you name the names of the men and women who teach these heresies and doctrines of demons all hell breaks out. One might ask why the difference? Why all the Christians fighting and debating with one another when a famous Christian is "named as a teacher of heresies?"

I want to say, a mild reaction happens with "exposure of false doctrines," and major reaction with exposing the name of a famous Charismatic Apostle? It seems strange so many would rather defend the name of the man, then defend the doctrines of the Bible. Here is the break down, naming names exposes an entire people group which identifies with the apostle or prophet which teaches the heresy. By naming the name of the false teacher it at the same time exposes those who agree with that deception. In effect you are saying to the Movement, as a group you are following a teacher who has led you into deception. So, naming a name brings focus upon the real issue of spiritual deception inside the Church. Let's face it no one likes to say they have been tricked or fooled by lies and deception. Especially, those who pride themselves in being more spiritual by having supernatural experiences.

So, pride and elitism come into play, especially when followers of a famous preacher has seduced them into a false premise of a superior position of "greater light, and esoteric hidden knowledge." Their pride would play out like, "I know what you don't know," I have the greater truth and you are just old school. However, who has convinced them of this superior truth, other than the man or woman who they follow. So those who are seduced to follow a false teacher must defend "the man," How do they defend? By using the Bible and the Scriptures as their evidence? Absolutely not! As heresies and false doctrines are exposed by the Scriptures. So, their argument is easily defeated by debating the Scriptures.

As those who follow heretical teachers are following the man, they must turn an accuse those who are confronting the false doctrines. So, when you name names of false teachers you will never get a repone about “proper doctrine.” Instead, you will hear this level of response: “you are creating division, you have no right to accuse the brethren, you are touching Gods anointed.” Who are you these men are doing so much good, you are a heresy hunter who is angry and unloving. Did you first go in private, as no one has all the truth, just spit out the chaff, and you are not Charismatic so you cant teach us about Charismatic practices.

Naming the names of false teachers leads the followers to attack those who are exposing them with “ad hominem” attacks meant to redirect the issue away from false doctrines, and upon the persons character and motives for calling out the false teacher. I have seen for years this very pattern happen dozens of times when naming false teachers by name. As the real issue is brought out, heresies and doctrines of demons are never really exposed, as the men who teach them are being protected by those Christians whom they have deceived.

2 Timothy 2:20-26
20 But in a great house there are not only vessels of
gold and of silver, but also of wood and of earth; and
some to honour, and some to dishonour.
21 If a man therefore purge himself from these, he shall
be a vessel unto honour, sanctified, and meet for the
master's use, and prepared unto every good work.
22 Flee also youthful lusts: but follow righteousness,
faith, charity, peace, with them that call on the Lord out
of a pure heart.
23 But foolish and unlearned questions avoid, knowing
that they do gender strifes.
24 And the servant of the Lord must not strive; but be
gentle unto all men, apt to teach, patient,
25 In meekness instructing those that oppose
themselves, if God peradventure will give them
repentance to the acknowledging of the truth.
26 And that they may recover themselves out of the
snare of the devil, who are taken captive by him at his
will.

In A Great House

What is Paul teaching in relationship to false teachers in the Church? A Great House means the Church, and the vessels used in the house are the workers, the different ministers who are called vessels in Pauli's example. Paul teaches vessels of gold and silver are approved of God and are vessels unto honor. While vessels of wood and earth are vessels of dishonor being compared to false teachers. If a worker in the Lords House purges himself by studying to show himself approved of God, he will purge himself from the practices of false teachers. A purged vessel in Gods house is meet for Gods use and prepared for every good work.

Paul exhorts Timothy to be this vessel of honor keeping moral purity, following righteousness, faith, love, peace with other vessels of honor who call upon the Lord out of a pure heart. Staying free from corrupting teachings which bring strife, and as far as possible kept at peace with all men. As the servant of the Lord must not strive, even when correcting those who are in deception. In meekness instructing those who have fallen from the truth, if God by your confrontation of deception will lead the deceived into repentance by acknowledging the truth.

What has happened to the vessels of dishonor who have fallen to teaching false doctrines? Satan has seduced them to believe doctrines of demons, leading the Church away from true faith in Christ into apostasy from the faith. Satan set a trap for false teachers into which they have fallen, not seeing they have been taken captive by their false teachings. In reality they have become pawns into the wicked schemes of Satan and are being used to do according to the will of Satan not knowing they are opposing God.

Chapter Three: Perilous Times

Perilous Times
2 Timothy 3:1
1 This know also, that in the last days perilous times shall come.

After Paul warns Timothy of the issues of false teachers and false doctrines in their days, Paul further develops the growing deception inside the Church in the last days. Paul calls the developers of end time deception "perilous times" warning the character of Christians and the Christian faith will be perverted with apostasy from the faith.

2 Timothy 3:2-5
2 For men shall be lovers of their own selves, covetous, boasters, proud, blasphemers, disobedient to parents, unthankful, unholy,
3 Without natural affection, trucebreakers, false accusers, incontinent, fierce, despisers of those that are good,
4 Traitors, heady, high minded, lovers of pleasures more than lovers of God;
5 Having a form of godliness, but denying the power thereof: from such turn away.

What many Christians might miss in this teaching is Pauls continuation of warning about corrupted Church leaders. The conditions listed seem to be a great violation from what Paul told Timothy in his first letter defining the qualifications of Church leaders. It appears those values are completely broken down inside the Church by godless leadership. One might think Paul has suddenly changed his topic from corrupt leaders and false doctrines because of the severity listed at the beginning of chapter three,. However, we must remember Paul did not put in Chapter divides when he wrote this letter to Timothy. As the result, chapter three is just a continuation of the same subject Paul was exposing to Timothy min chapter two. What is truly alarming is Pauls predictions of the moral and character decay of leadership inside the organized Church in the last days.

Not only leaders but the Church membership as a whole will face moral godless decay as it moves towards an end-time apostasy. Christians living in these last days will have to be vigilant in their own moral commitments and test the spirits of their Christian leaders.

Paul instructs Timothy to watch over his doctrines, and to help contend for the faith by calling upon those who serve the Lord out of a pure heart of devotion. For those who character fails the test of qualifications for Church leadership, Christians must hold strict standards and not tolerate such character and behaviors. For such corrupted Church leaders all must turn away.

Christians Living In Perilous Times
We live in days which the Bible describes as "perilous times." What does that exactly mean as the Greek Word for perilous is "chalepos" in English meaning dangerous or fierce. What Christians must realize the melt down which is increasing on earth, an increase in lawlessness. Which will push Christians to move away from their love for Jesus Christ, and their love for one another. In 2 Timothy the last days peril is spelled out so Christians can fight the good fight of faith and keep true in the Lord as conditions continue to corrupt.

The first condition listed which creates a great peril for the Christian faith is "love of self." Notice how the order of the Commandments is to love the Lord your God first and foremost. However, in the last days men will choose the "self-life, self-centered, self-willed, self-exalting, while holding "a form of godliness." A man centered self-love world will attempt to invade the last days Church, filling the Church with man centered philosophies.

Look where self-love leads, away from God into selfish pursuits. "Covetous," the lust and desires from the things of this world. A willingness to hate, abuse, and murder to get them. Look how men are willing to burn down their own cities in a sense of "self-entitlement." Men who call good evil, and evil good. Despisers of those who are truly good, and truthful, and law abiding. Hate, abuse, rage, and violence will fill the earth, and much of that evil will be directed towards the authentic Church of Jesus Christ, and the Jewish peoples.

Mankind without a conscience, who have hardened their hearts in willful defiance of God and His moral laws. Are you looking for increased justice, and protection by law as a Christian in a world which is growing in its hatred of God and the Church? Men will sell their souls to evil, traitors who will betray even those of their own families. A growing generational divide where Children are being "indoctrinated with godless beliefs. Who become their own little self-serving gods? Parental authority is being stripped away as children "judge their own parents" as old fashioned and out of touch with modern cultural values. A generation of entitled sons and daughter who are filled with "educational propaganda" which has taught them to celebrate an immoral lifestyle. Producing a self-absorbed generation who has become a completely Bible ignorant generation. Who hold to a spirituality, but have abandoned an "absolute moral truth, for moral relativism. Who reject Jesus Christ as the only way, and declare all religions demonstrate the way to God?

Distraction abounds in a world of perilous times. As so much darkness rises, many influences will come to vey for your time and attention. As lack will become one of the main topics for surviving, culture will become more fearful and aggressive. We see when a nation falls to lack and there is not enough food to supply the culture.

Or the financial security which they depend on falls to the ground, and they have no way to buy, not enough to pay for living expenses. Look at the effects of "war," starvation, loss of family, loss of homes, no way to continue is employment. Now consider wars and rumours of wars, people groups hating one another. Notice the rise of inner-city violence and murder, then extending out in racial hate and ethnic cleansings.

The world as we have known it is quickly changing moving towards greater instability, and the moving of the masses of peoples into fear, hate, rage. A perilous time where mankind has lost natural affection, living for themselves, at the expense of others. A culture of lies, where the truth is repressed, and lies are used as a weapon against the truth. Do you think as a Christian you will not be touched by the perilous times in which we live? By the time you come to your senses, your loss before God will be very great. Playing Church and living in the fantasy of false doctrines which deny the perilous times is one of the grand deceptions of Church in these days. Being distracted with all the problems, the lack of security, and the inability to fix the circumstances you find yourself. Why do the Scriptures warn of the Great Falling Away from the faith, as times grow dark many will be disillusioned with God. Even now we see many Christians who were formerly passionate for the Lord walking away, going back into living for themselves.

What Is the Great Apostasy?

In Paul's day the Christians of the Church of Thessalonians felt they had missed the first rapture and were left behind to face the Tribulation. However, the apostle Paul made a distinction between the suffering of the first century saints under Roman persecution, and the coming Tribulation. Apostle Paul noted the Tribulation time had not yet come, as the Great apostasy, the falling away from the faith was to coordinate with this time.

Now through the Church age there has been a great deal of departure from the authentic Christian faith. One of the major contributing factors was the rise of Catholicism and the Catholic Church. When Emperor Constantine declared Christianity to be the religion of the state, pagan principles were incorporated by the Church of Rome into the Christian faith. In this way the paganism of the Christian faith has existed for over 1500 years. This, however, is not the Great Falling Away which Paul was teaching about in Thessalonica. Instead, this is the generalized attack of Christian doctrine, and departure from the orthodoxy of the original apostles teaching.

Today we have Protestant versions of doctrinal departure, and the introduction of man-made traditions, and human philosophy. In this way the authentic Christian faith has been attacked for a long time over the centuries by Protestant denominations also. Church history has proven what Jesus Christ warned is happened. The wheat and tares will grow side-by side during the Church age until the time of harvest at the end of the age. It is at the time of Tribulation the harvest will begin, where the wheat will be separated out from the tares by rapture and resurrection. It is also during the time of Tribulation which Paul speaks a great worldwide departure from the faith will occur called the Great Falling Away. Here are the passages which inform us of the Great End time Apostasy.

2 Thessalonians 2:1-3
1 Now we beseech you, brethren, by the coming of our Lord Jesus Christ, and by our gathering together unto him,
2 That ye be not soon shaken in mind, or be troubled, neither by spirit, nor by word, nor by letter as from us, as that the day of Christ is at hand.
3 Let no man deceive you by any means: for that day shall not come, except there comes a falling away first, and that man of sin be revealed, the son of perdition.

What leads Christians into the Great Apostasy

The Scriptures warn of great end time deception which leads the Church into the Great Apostasy. By its very definition apostasy can only be committed by those who first believed and then turned from the faith. So,

Christians who have made a faith commitment to Jesus Christ, and then turned away from the faith, and even denying the Lord is the sin of apostasy. In the last days, the pressure to apostatize from the faith will become very great. Conditions from both inside the Church and outside the Church will lead Christians away into apostate conditions.
The apostle Paul in many of his writings speaks and warns of end time deception and apostasy. Paul said the influences from inside the Church will come from 1) false teachers, 2) Doctrines of demons, and 3) Immorality in the lives of Christians.

1 Timothy 4:1-2
1 Now the Spirit speaketh expressly, that in the latter times some shall depart from the faith, giving heed to seducing spirits, and doctrines of devils.
2 Speaking lies in hypocrisy; having their conscience seared with a hot iron.

In this passage the influences come from corrupted leaders who teach Christians manmade wisdom, doctrines which deny the faith which come from evil spirits. The seducing spirits are the teachers themselves who seek to use the Church from the own personal profit and gain.

Again, in Paul's second letter to Timothy, the issue of end time peril is brought to the forefront. Paul includes how evil men and imposters have invaded the Church whose immorality is corrupting the household of faith. Paul uses the definition of perilous times as the Christian faith is being drawn away by corrupted leaders, false doctrines, and immoral practices. Paul teaches the leaders will be self-seeking, conceited, lifted with pride, having a form of godliness, but deny the power of sanctified living. These types of leaders are bound by lust and greed, having a love of pleasure more than a love of God.

These types of leaders are those who have their conscience seared as with a hot iron. Play acting the faith in hypocrisy, but this sort is creeping around seeking to beguile unstable souls by committing acts of immorality. While they continue to feast with you at the Lords table.

Leaders who have been shown the truth but have turned aside, every learning but not willing to live in the truth. Men who are opposed to the Holy Spirit, and some even walk-in demonic powers. They are resisting the truth, men of corruption, reprobate concerning the faith.

Ironically, Paul warns the Church of the last days will welcome evil men and imposters who are willing to itch their ears with Christian philosophy. These philosophies deny the doctrines of the faith and lead the Church into apostasy. Paul warns in the last days, Christians will not endure sound doctrines, but will instead heap to themselves corrupted teachers who will tell them the philosophical lies they want to hear.

2 Timothy 3:5-13
5 Having a form of godliness but denying the power
thereof: from such turn away.
6 For of this sort are they which creep into houses, and
lead captive silly women laden with sins, led away with
divers' lusts,
7 Ever learning, and never able to come to the
knowledge of the truth.
8 Now as Jannes and Jambres withstood Moses, so do
these also resist the truth: men of corrupt minds,
reprobate concerning the faith.
9 But they shall proceed no further: for their folly shall
be manifest unto all men, as theirs also was.
10 But thou hast fully known my doctrine, manner of
life, purpose, faith, long suffering, charity, patience,
11 Persecutions, afflictions, which came unto me at
Antioch, at Iconium, at Lystra; what persecutions I
endured: but out of them all the Lord delivered me.
12 Yea, and all that will live godly in Christ Jesus shall
suffer persecution.
13 But evil men and seducers shall wax worse and
worse, deceiving, and being deceived.

Jesus Christ also warned Christians of end times deception including false Christs, false prophets, and lying signs and wonders. Also, the conditions of the world will be like the days of Noah before the great flood, and wide scale acceptance of sexual immorality like in the time of Lot and Sodom.

Matthew 24:37-39
37 But as the days of Noe were, so shall also the coming
of the Son of man be.
38 For as in the days that were before the flood they
were eating and drinking, marrying and giving in
marriage, until the day that Noe entered the ark,
39 And knew not until the flood came, and took them all
away; so, shall also the coming of the Son of man be.

What was Jesus Christ warning the Church to avoid? The last days will be filled with a spirit of lawlessness where men have abandoned all fear of God and are continuously breaking the laws of God. As the result of lawlessness abounding, the love of many Christians will grow cold as the pressures to compromise the faith are increased. It will seem God is doing nothing about the perversion which has grown upon the earth, and mankind seems to get away with sin and wickedness. The influences of a corrupted world, an immoral culture, will press Christians to compromise with the world.

Luke 21:34-36
34 And take heed to yourselves, lest at any time your
hearts be overcharged with surfeiting, and drunkenness,
and cares of this life, and so that day come upon you
unawares.
35 For as a snare shall it come on all them that dwell on
the face of the whole earth.

36 Watch ye therefore, and pray always, that ye may be accounted worthy to escape all these things that shall come to pass, and to stand before the Son of man.

What is Jesus Christ warning His disciples to watch and pray for? To escape the end times deception and trials which are coming upon the whole world, as a snare to capture every man into Satanic deception. When the cares of this life, the deceitfulness of riches, and the lusts of worldly things can enter the Christian who is not watching and choke his faith. In order to escape the end time deception which leads the Church into the Great Apostasy, the saints must watch and pray to be counted worthy to escape. Where is the escape, by rapture to stand before the Lord?

End time apostasy and deception is well documented in Scriptures by multiple original apostolic teachers who speak of end time peril. Let a man take heed to these warnings as the days which this book is being written are lawless times and the time of Tribulation is drawing near. Are we not seeing the great lawless spirit leading the world into denying Jesus Christ? Are there not evidences the Church is in a major departure from the authority of Scriptures, and Bible morality? Are not the last days which are perilous, now set before us? Take heed to yourselves lest any man think he stands untouched by these corrupting influences. Take heed, watch, and pray lest you fall.

Paul Compares His Life

Paul then contrasts then his life of service to Jesus Christ in comparison to corrupt Church leaders. Paul says to Timothy you have seen my life as an open book with nothing hidden in hypocrisy. Paul says you have fully known my doctrine, the character by which I have conducted my ministry, and the great cost to my own life to stay faithful in service to Jesus Christ. Paul then gives actual cities and times and events of those persecutions to demonstrate the difference with those who are lovers of themselves.
Paul reaffirms all those who hold to the true character of Jesus Christ are going to suffer persecution. For instead of the world getting better all the time evil men and imposters wax worse and worse leading the Church astray. Paul says of Timothy, but you continue in the sound doctrines being assured from who you have learned them.

Paul then approves of Timothy's knowledge of the written word of God having studied the Scriptures from his childhood. Paul says Timothy has been made wise in Christ having studied the Scriptures making him wise in the ways of the Lord. Paul the confirms Timothy can stand on the infallibility of Gods, and was given to Gods holy apostles and prophets by inspiration. For by the infallible word of God, is profitable for doctrine, for reproof, for correction and for training in righteousness. That Gods approved Church leaders may be perfect, or mature in Christ. Leading to a great future reward being thoroughly furnished to perform good works in truth and godliness.

2 Timothy 3:10-17
10 But thou hast fully known my doctrine, manner of
life, purpose, faith, longsuffering, charity, patience,
11 Persecutions, afflictions, which came unto
me at Antioch, at Iconium, at Lystra; what persecutions I
endured: but out of them all the Lord delivered me.
12 Yea, and all that will live godly in Christ Jesus shall
suffer persecution.
13 But evil men and seducers shall wax worse and
worse, deceiving, and being deceived.
14 But continue thou in the things which thou hast
learned and hast been assured of, knowing of
whom thou hast learned them;
15 And that from a child thou hast known the
holy scriptures, which are able to make thee wise unto
salvation through faith which is in Christ Jesus.
16 All scripture is given by inspiration of
God, and is profitable for doctrine, for reproof, for corre
ction, for instruction in righteousness:
17 That the man of God may
be perfect, thoroughly unto all good works

Chapter Four: Preach the Word

2 Timothy 4:1-2
I charge thee therefore before God, and the Lord
Jesus Christ, who shall judge the quick and the
dead at his appearing and his kingdom;
2 Preach the word; be instant in season, out of
season; reprove, rebuke, exhort with all long
suffering and doctrine.

After Paul affirming Timothy's knowledge of Scriptures, and the value of Gods infallible Scriptures, Paul charges Timothy to preach the word. God will judge the living and dead at His appearing holding the saints accountability to His word and His will. When Jesus Christ appears, He will bring the Kingdom of Heaven with Him. For the Lord God will test the quality of every man's works according to His word. For these reasons Paul charges for Timothy to preach the doctrines of Jesus Christ when it appears convenient, or in times when one might suffer persecution. In preaching the doctrines of Jesus Christ it's not with smooth speech or great swelling words of vanity, instead reprove, exhort and rebuke with true doctrines and correction. Warn mankind and the church with all long suffering, and authentic doctrines of Jesus Christ.

What Is Authentic Preaching

Why is it important to test the spirit of our leaders and teachers? The true reason is to hold them accountable for what they are teaching. Without our Church leaders being held accountable to the authority of Scriptures, the Church can be led into dangerous waters. The apostle Paul was very active in all his writings warning of false doctrines and apostasy from the faith.

Notice how pure doctrine speaks to a man's heart, for out of the heart comes the issues of life. When your heart is wrong, your conscience is defiled with sin. Sometimes a person's conscience is so defiled with sin the person has a seared heart deeply repressing the truth of Gods commandments. The true doctrines of Christ call for a pure heart, a good conscience before God, and a genuine faith which is an open book before all men.

When Christians put away the doctrines of Jesus Christ, they are not holding fast to the faith. As they oppose Gods Word their conscience is defiled not willing to listen to the Holy Spirits conviction. In this condition their walk in the Lord has steered off course and will be deeply damaged by ship wreck if continued on this course. Church leaders who have hardened their hearts to the true doctrines of Christ and teach doctrines of demons are putting the Church in danger. Without confrontation and correction of deception in the lives of our Church leaders, Satan will gain a great advantage. As doctrines of demons and seducing spirits will have free reign leading the whole Church apostasy from the faith.

1 Timothy 1:5
[5] Now the end of the commandment is charity out of a pure heart, and of a good conscience, and of faith unfeigned:

1 Timothy 1:19-20
[19] Holding faith, and a good conscience; which some having put away concerning faith have made shipwreck:
[20] Of whom is Hymenaeus and Alexander; whom I have delivered unto Satan, that they may learn not to blaspheme.

In order for the true standards of preaching and teaching to be accomplished all man-made opinions and philosophy should be put to the Cross. No man or woman has the right to stand up and speak in the name of the Lord, and then speak of their own opinions and philosophy. Real preaching and teaching will be confrontational in nature where reproof and correction are common. For a man's life is confronted by the doctrines of Jesus Christ, as the Life of Christ demands our surrender. All manner of lies, sin, and deception are brought out into the light by true preaching the doctrines of Jesus Christ.

For every man called by God to preach or teach, a charge has been given to speak the Word of God in truth. Real preaching is exhortative in nature but is not entertainment. Real preaching is done in the power of the Holy Spirit and should convict a man's conscience. Instead of speaking human philosophies which are feel good or popular opinion, will smooth a man's conscience even though the man is not right with God. Real preaching has elements of reproof, even rebuke which are directed to expose a man's true-life rebuking all lies, deception, and sinful practices. When a man comes to a true Bible preacher his conscience should be reproved and rebuked by the authority of Scriptures. Being warned of the consequences of sin both now and at the future judgment at the Second Coming of Jesus Christ.

Without true Biblical preaching the whole of the Church can fall into an apostate condition where Christians have departed from the faith. Paul warns of this peril in the days we live, where Christians won't want their lives confronted and their actions rebuked. Instead, will gather to themselves teachers who tell them the manmade philosophies they want to hear. Modern preachers will not confront the Church of their sins and worldly living, instead will approve of Christians in compromise. Today a real Gospel preacher be could accused of as a "prophet of doom," or a religious Pharisee. As the Christian crowd has heaped to themselves an abundance of false apostles and prophets who tickle their ears. Is it any wonder without real Gospel preachers many people simply see the Church as nonessential in real life?

2 Timothy 4:3-4
3 For the time will come when they
will not endure sound doctrine; but after their
own lusts shall they heap to
themselves teachers, having itching ears;
4 And they shall turn away their ears from the
truth, and shall be turned unto fables

Paul warns Timothy the Church will fall away from the faith refusing to hear sound doctrines and instead choosing to hear Christian fables in its place. Not only refusing the true doctrines of Jesus Christ, instead choosing a false Gospel based upon manmade philosophies. To eliminate the true doctrines of Jesus Christ, an end times Church moving into apostasy will heap unto themselves Church leaders who will itch their ears telling them the Christian fables they only want to hear.

Not Wanting To Hear

If you're a Christian you may have seen how your unsaved family and friends are resistant to hearing the Gospel. They simply don't want you telling them something they don't want to hear. The truth which you carry is a matter of life and death, but they would rather risk eternal damnation than hear what you have to say. There is a real life problem in the world where Satan has blinded the minds of the unbelieving lest they should receive the Glorious Gospel of Jesus Christ. A true problem exists not wanting to hear from God what could change your life forever. Sin has blinded the condition of their hearts effecting their ability to receive the truth and be saved.

Now let's apply this situation of not wanting to hear the truth to Christians. The Scriptures teach one of the primary issues among the saved in Christ, is not having the willingness to hear the complete council of the Lord. Of course, the dark ages demonstrate the gross departure from the authority of Scriptures unto the traditions and manmade doctrines which has dominated the Church for over a thousand years. Trying to lead a Christian out of false doctrines and beliefs is no simple task. All over the world today false doctrines and teachers are leading Christians astray by doctrines of demons and seducing spirits. When a Christian comes under the deception of a false doctrine evil spirits are involved in drawing the saint away from the true doctrines of Christ. The stronghold has the power to close down the person from hearing the truth. So one of the primary issues of spiritual warfare among Christians is shutting down their ability to hear the truth.

Even now, there are some doctrines which are celebrated as the truth which are right out of the pit of Hell. Even though a deceived Christian can be confronted by Scriptures, it appears they would rather choose to have their ears itched by a false teacher who is willing to them the lies they want to hear. Christian fables of which they want to hear. Itching ears, a unwillingness to hear the true doctrines of Christ have led millions of Christians to their favorite false teachers. The Bible has warned of these days when Christians will have stopped hungering for the Word of God, and will heap to themselves teachers according to their lusts having itching ears, and turn to Christian fables.

Today the Church is full of story tellers who would rather profit off the Church than to confront the Church with the true doctrines of Christ. The Christian story tellers preach their Christian fables to the emotions of man, so men can feel good about themselves. A man living in sin who has compromised his walk with the Lord can go to Church and sooth his conscience by a compromised message of love, and a no judgment God who accepts you as you are. The Church is rarely confronted in her sin, or a call for repentance, and turning from sin back to the Lord. This message of the Love of God without a Cross and without consequences has dominated the pulpit for over a decade. It has led men to believe in a no future judgment of God false Gospel.

If you were tell the typical modern day Christian God will judge them for the way they have lived after coming into saving faith in Christ, many would accuse you of being legalistic, old school, sin conscience, or a religious

Pharisee, even a heretic. A modern Christian has been taught to close their ears to future accountability and judgment. Will Christ cause a Christian to suffer loss at the Judgment Seat of Christ? Absolutely according to Scriptures. Can a Christian be judged as a reprobate, and lose the right to future entrance into the Kingdom of Heaven? Can a Christian so bury their talent from God to be judged a wicked and unprofitable servant? Can the judgment upon such a Christian cause them to forfeit the coming Kingdom of Heaven? Can the same wicked servant of the Lord be cast into outer darkness where there is weeping and gnashing of teeth? All these warnings are clear from Scriptures, "he who has ears to hear what the Spirit is saying to the Church."

When Words Have Lost Their Value

We live in a day where words have lost their value. As a man's words are only as good as the person who stands behind them. So we live in a day where words can just be emptying sayings, with no real value or character behind them. The world is filling up with meaningless words spoken but are just becoming all the empty noise and chatter which are filling up the air waves. Since what is being spoken has little value it's getting harder for persons to discern what is truly valuable in life. I have found smooth speech and enticing words have their ability to attract the masses. However, words which carry weight and substance are difficult to listen too, as they require more investment from our lives. What is the problem today? People have a tough time listening to the truth.

Want to see how the world is going full circle back into the temptation of the Garden of Eden? For all that is in the world is the lust of the flesh, the lust of the eyes, and the pride of life. Satan has for centuries ever since the fall used the vanity of empty lies and deception to get men to take his bate. A flood tide of words now fill up the days, and men have taken the bait and are lost to same temptations Adam and Eve failed in. The Bible commands the saints to love not the world as those very same lusts and pride have now become normalized throughout the world systems. Christians must now be very careful to watch over their hearts as to what you listen has become a life and death matter. Mankind is listening to the Father of Lies in whom there is no truth. For when he speaks he speaks a lie for there is no truth in him.

Why are people so committed to speak things which are not true? Why are people so investing their time, their talents, their life into empty pursuits which are based upon lies and deception. The answer is simple Satan is flooding the world with all manner of talk so as to shut out the Gospel. How often do you hear someone speak of the Gospel, or talk with regularity the Scriptures as the way, the truth, the life? How little is the Gospel permitted in everyday conversations, and when a Christian begins to speak out many simply will close their ears and are not willing to listen. They can listen to all manner of empty vanity, but when the eternal words of God are spoken they run and hide from the eternal truth.

Don't think the practice of running from Gods word is just outside the Church. Today we have right inside the household of God empty meaningless words spoken as Gods truth. Why is there so much vanity accepted as God speaking in today's Church? The Bible warns in the last days men will depart from wanting to hear the eternal sound doctrines of Jesus Christ. Instead Christians will be drawn to men who tell them the vanity they want to hear. Christians who have itching ears and have closed themselves off from the deep character and substance of the Gospel, and instead choose fairy tales which itch their ears with vain philosophies. Look at today's Church world filled with memes and Christian entertainment. How little are the saints corrected by the confrontation of sin, and challenged to pick up the Cross in self-denial to follow the Lord. A false Gospel of teaching you can have the worlds goods and way of living are openly preached. Just look at how the warnings of Scriptures are ignored which direct the saints to keep oneself unspotted from the world.

Why are the false prophets so adhered to even when the volume of false prophecies is exposed year after year. Why is the Church being led by men and women who won't preach the Gospel, won't teach the doctrines of Christ? Who use smooth speech and alluring words which appeal to the flesh, and actually drawn men away from Christ and unto themselves. Why do Christians follow the false prophets, it's simple, they heap voices who tell them lies they want to believe. A simple test of prophetic words by the Scriptures would prove how hollow, how empty are their boasts. Based upon the world's values and the glorification of man the false prophet's allure by the lusts of the flesh. Few are the Christians who cry out against the empty words of the prophets.

Conclusion: Pauls Final Words

Paul wants to see Timothy once again before Paul's departure in death, so asking Timothy to do due diligence to come quickly. Paul gives a testimony of being forsaken by Delmas who likely feared for his own life in Rome and the threat of prison or martyrdom. Other team members had departed to other locations leaving Paul alone with only Luke the physician remaining.
Paul has changed his mind about Mark who had abandoned Paul years ago while fearing persecution. Timothy was now to bring Mark with him, as Paul had recognized how much Mark had changed from those earlier days. Paul wanted his books and writings to be brought to him in jail. One of Pauls persecutors is named by name, Alexander the copper smith. Paul suffered greatly by Alexander insomuch all others fled leaving Paul alone in the face of great suffering. Paul then gives witness of how God stood with Paul to keep him from the mouth of the lion. The Lord keep Paul through life and death circumstances until all Pauls days should be fulfilled.

What happens when relationships which are very important break down and fail? The human experience is enriched by beneficial relationships counted as family and good friends. How difficult is a relationship in which you have given your trust, and then breaks down and fails. Often circumstances which come about under great pressure and trials lead to fracturing and splitting of relational bonds. The pressure cooker of circumstances often leads to a break down in natural human love often leading to fracture and betrayal.

The apostle Paul had many co laborers in the Gospel, and many were fellow apostles who travelled with Paul. However, many times these same men risked their lives as Paul was often in the middle of uprisings of citizens. In this case a copper smith named Alexander brought great persecution to Pauls life, to the point Pauls companions feared relating to Paul in those circumstances. Note Pauls personal testimony during that time, “all men forsake me.” Paul must face this battle alone without the strength of his ministry team, in a sense a betrayal in a time of great need. Paul prayed that it would not be held against them when the Lord judged their actions.

Notice Paul did not do anything wrong, instead was willing to suffer unto death in preaching the Gospel to the Gentiles where God would lead. It’s one thing for people who you love to give up on you because of all the problems of wrongdoing. It’s a completely different issue when in love you suffer loss for doing what is right. In this case Pauls thorn could have been betrayal having to suffer by himself in complete dependence upon the Lord.

In this way many others can relate to being betrayed by others who fail to walk in love. This is common in life relationships are often defined by betrayal and our responses. Notice the ultimate betrayal of Jesus Christ at the Cross. Where men who were companions of the Lord fled in fear for their own lives. Perhaps walking with the Lord brings about great suffering from the many relationships which have the potential to fail, with a man or woman who will not compromise their walk with the Lord.

Betrayal is often defined by another experience of complete aloneness's called abandonment. Probably one of life's great issues of suffering is feeling all alone being abandoned with no one to turn for relief or comfort. To demonstrate the depth of suffering in abandonment the Scriptures record Jesus Christs experience on the Cross.

Psalm 22:1-2
1 My God, my God, why hast thou forsaken me? why art thou so far from helping me, and from the words of my roaring?
2 O my God, I cry in the daytime, but thou hearest not; and in the night season, and am not silent.

Is not one of life's greatest betrayals leading to feeling alone with no one being by your side. Many feel alone and abandoned by God in times of great betrayal. "My God My God why have you forsaken me?" This must be the question which comes from the lips of billions of peoples who are suffering the injustices of an evil fallen world of sin and death. Where is a God of love when so much evil is present in this world?

2 Timothy 4:14-18
14 Alexander the coppersmith did me much evil: the
Lord reward him according to his works:
15 Of whom be thou ware also; for he hath greatly
withstood our words.
16 At my first answer no man stood with me, but all
men forsook me: I pray God that it may not be laid
to their charge.
17 Notwithstanding the Lord stood with me, and
strengthened me; that by me the preaching might
be fully known, and that all the Gentiles might hear:
and I was delivered out of the mouth of the lion.
18 And the Lord shall deliver me from every evil
work, and will preserve me unto his heavenly
kingdom: to whom be glory for ever and ever.
Amen.

Once again Paul speaks of the coming Kingdom of Heaven age which Paul would be rewarded as a faithful witness for Jesus Christ. Understanding Pauls final words must include an understanding of the coming Kingdom of Heaven age.

Saints Must Qualify to Rule with Christ

Christians can qualify to rule with Jesus Christ in the Kingdom of heaven age. You are in a race to finish the course to win a prize, an imperishable crown. Paul called the prize of the high calling the right to rule and reign with Jesus Christ in the next age. Paul said if he did not bring his body into subjection, he would be disapproved, a reprobate, one not qualified. Now was Paul to be cast away from his salvation, after having suffered so much for the faith? Absolutely not, Paul was speaking of not obtaining the Crown, being disqualified at the Judgment Seat of Christ not qualifying for Kingdom of Heaven age right to rule.

1 Corinthians 9:24-27
24 Know ye not that they which run in a race run all, but one receiveth the prize? So run, that ye may obtain.
25 And every man that striveth for the mastery is temperate in all things. Now they do it to obtain a corruptible crown; but we an incorruptible.
26 I therefore so run, not as uncertainly; so fight I, not as one that beateth the air:
27 But I keep under my body, and bring it into subjection: lest that by any means, when I have preached to others, I myself should be a castaway.

The prize of the high calling is the right of being crowned. A King Priest, an immortal saint, who qualifies for the first resurrection obtaining the Kingdom age as a qualified son of God. Many today in the modern Church attempt to boast of a crown they have not yet attained, and a kingship in which they have no throne. Many Christians are attempting to display an authority, and power which demonstrates they are already kings in this present evil age. As the result of the lack of true kingship, all manner of “prophetic decrees,” are made to declare their false kingship, and kingdom. Others display fantasy spiritual warfare games, even holding court in heaven to bring Satan to trial. They have “invented practices” which are not the true government of God. They are not kings seated upon heavenly thrones executing the government of God throughout the earth. Their kingdom is one of the flesh, self-declared, a religious game, which refuses to pick up the Cross in self-denial fellowshipping in the sufferings of Christ. They are in effect disqualifying themselves by not running “legally,” they have yet to finish the race, yet want to declare the prize of the victor.

The Crown and Throne of the Kingdom is not given until the end of the age. To this purpose Jesus Christ was abundantly clear. Jesus Christ said the throne, the right to rule in the Kingdom age would only be given to those saints who were willing to pay full price now. You must surrender all to Jesus Christ now in authentic devotion, committing all to Him in service willing to count all things lost. This is what Jesus Christ meant when He commanded His disciples to “seek first the Kingdom, and His righteousness.”

Matthew 19:27-30

27 Then answered Peter and said unto him, Behold, we have forsaken all, and followed thee; what shall we have therefore?

28 And Jesus said unto them, Verily I say unto you, That
ye which have followed me, in the regeneration when
the Son of man shall sit in the throne of his glory, ye also
shall sit upon twelve thrones, judging the twelve tribes
of Israel.
29 And every one that hath forsaken houses, or
brethren, or sisters, or father, or mother, or wife, or
children, or lands, for my name's sake, shall receive an
hundredfold, and shall inherit everlasting life.
30 But many that are first shall be last; and the last shall
be first.

Peter was seeking the Kingdom the right to rule with Jesus Christ, however before then Peter was required to give all to Jesus Christ. “Behold we have forsaken all, and followed you, what shall we have therefore?” (Matthew 19:27). In the regeneration, and the time which Christ returns the coming transformation into the Kingdom age, “when the Son of Man shall sit in the Throne of His glory,” (future event), you (Peter) shall be rewarded with “your own Throne.” (Future) For today is the day of qualification, and everyone who has forsaken houses, brothers, sisters, or fathers, or mothers, or wife, or children, or lands, for the sake of Jesus Christ shall inherit the Crown and Throne. For the Kingdom age is given by inheritance only to the qualified.

Now comes the true recognition of Jesus Christs warning; not everyone who says to Me Lord, Lord shall enter the Kingdom of heaven. For many will come to Me on that day (Day of Judgment) and say to Me Lord did we not prophesy in your name, in your name work mighty miracles, and in your name cast out evil spirits? I will say to you “depart from Me you workers of iniquity” These Christians attempted to win the Crown by taking the things of God and using them for themselves. They did not run the race in a lawful way and were disqualified from the crown. All their pretense play acting as if they were great kings failed them at the Judgment. It cost them the real Crown and Kingdom Age Throne. Imposters and pretenders who are “being crowned by manmade glorification,” have their “reward now.” A perishable crown of man's glory, which is quickly fading, disqualifying them for the next age. Fake kings now with manufactured self-serving kingdoms.

2 Timothy 4:9-22
9 Do thy diligence to come shortly unto me:
10 For Demas hath forsaken me, having
loved this present world, and is
departed unto Thessalonica; Crescens to Galatia, Titus u
nto Dalmatia.
11 Only Luke is with me. Take Mark, and bring him with
thee: for he is profitable to me for the ministry.
12 And Tychicus have I sent to Ephesus.
13 The cloke that I left at Troas with Carpus, when thou
comest, bring with thee, and the books, but
especially the parchments
14 Alexander the coppersmith did me much evil: the
Lord reward him according to his works:

15 Of whom be thou ware also; for he
hath greatly withstood our words.
16 At my first answer no man stood
with me, but all men forsook me: I pray God that it
may not be laid to their charge.
17 Notwithstanding the Lord stood with
me, and strengthened me; that by me the
preaching might be fully known, and that all the
Gentiles might hear: and I was delivered out of the
mouth of the lion.
18 And the Lord shall
deliver me from every evil work, and will
preserve me unto his heavenly kingdom: to
whom be glory for ever and ever. Amen.
19 Salute Prisca and Aquila, and the household of
Onesiphorus.
20 Erastus abode at Corinth: but Trophimus have I
left at Miletum sick.
21 Do thy diligence to
come before winter. Eubulus greeteth thee, and Pudens
, and Linus, andClaudia, and all the brethren.
22 The
Lord Jesus Christ be with thy spirit. Grace be with you. A
men.

Apostle Pauls final words are some directions concerning fellow laborers. Paul wants Timothy to come before winter and gives greetings from some brethren in Rome. Paul blesses Timothy with a blessing of the Lord's presence. Finally, calls God's grace be with

Timothy as Paul knows without God's grace all is in vain. Paul's prayer ends with, "so be it."

Pauls
Thorn In
the Flesh
Don Pirozok

Apostasy then is a turning away from Jesus Christ and denying the faith which was once delivered unto you. Apostasy in the Christian faith can only be committed by Christians who were truly born again. Now a great many have believed Christians cannot commit the sin of apostasy. Their reasoning is once you are born again the Lord will keep you and never forsake you. So, if one who professed a relationship with Jesus Christ then turns from that relationship, they reason this person was never really saved in the first place. Others confess the sin of apostasy is damnable leading to Christians who are born again to lose their salvation. I trust many Scriptures are brought forth which demonstrates their position. However, there can only be one real Scriptural truth about Christians in apostasy. We must set aside our prejudice and examine more fully what happens to Christians in apostasy.
Christians In Apostasy
Don Pirozak
Christians
In
Apostasy
Don Pirozak

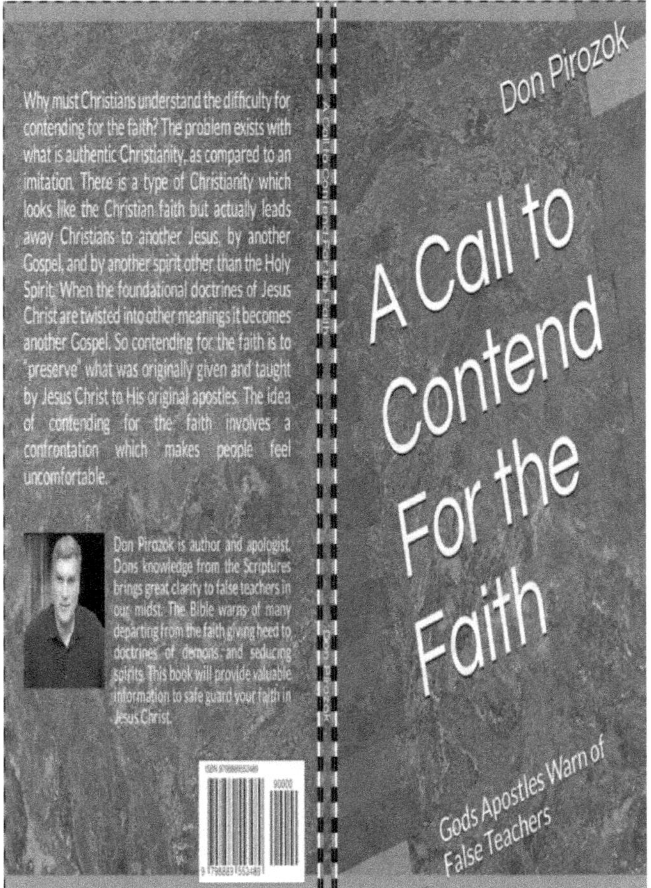
Why must Christians understand the difficulty for contending for the faith? The problem exists with what is authentic Christianity, as compared to an imitation. There is a type of Christianity which looks like the Christian faith but actually leads away Christians to another Jesus, by another Gospel, and by another spirit other than the Holy Spirit. When the foundational doctrines of Jesus Christ are twisted into other meanings it becomes another Gospel. So contending for the faith is to "preserve" what was originally given and taught by Jesus Christ to His original apostles. The idea of contending for the faith involves a confrontation which makes people feel uncomfortable.
Don Pirozok is author and apologist. Dons knowledge from the Scriptures brings great clarity to false teachers in our midst. The Bible warns of many departing from the faith giving heed to doctrines of demons and seducing spirits. This book will provide valuable information to safe guard your faith in Jesus Christ.
Don Pirozok
A Call to Contend For the Faith
Gods Apostles Warn of False Teachers

In writing of our common salvation Paul speaks of our three positions in the Christian faith 1) Our heavenly position where the saints are seated with Christ 2) Our walk by faith in the Spirit in this present evil age 3) Standing against the wiles of the Devil in spiritual warfare. Paul will break down these three positions and take us through how to see and live in them as born-again sons of God.
Seated with Christ
Don Pirozok is author and apologist. Dons knowledge from the Scriptures brings great clarity to spiritual issues in our day. The Book of Ephesians is one of the most spiritual letters given to the Church. This book will provide valuable information to safe guard your faith in Jesus Christ.
Don Pirozok
Seated with Christ
An Overview of Book of Ephesians
Don Pirozok

www.ingramcontent.com/pod-product-compliance
Lightning Source LLC
LaVergne TN
LVHW050342160826
845677LV00014B/3741

* 9 7 9 8 8 9 1 4 5 4 1 1 8 *